DISCOVERING GRACE IN DESPAIR

Finding hope in Christ when all hope seems gone

DIANNA (MOFFITT) CARROLL

DMC Publishing

I would like to dedicate this devotional to all my family who have supported and encouraged me every step of the way.

CONTENTS

FOREWORD

"My grace is sufficient for you, for my power is made perfect in weakness." (2 Corinthians 12:9) Paul often penned his letters to the church during profound moments of suffering and pain. Likewise, we can read many of David's life struggles in his psalms. While hiding in caves or grieving over his sins, David allows us to see how a believer can struggle with despair. It is in these dark moments that the clutter of our lives fades to the background. When we feel that we are at the end of our rope, the gospel reminds us that God's grace is a gift. The struggle for many who find themselves feeling trapped is believing what we know is true.

This devotional is not just sound biblical truth, but words salted with compassion and grace. Each chapter is written from Dianna's journey through pain, loss, and suffering. Her experience in counseling as a pastor's wife offers a unique perspective that many will find refreshing. The greatest encouragement from this little book will be how you will learn to see and savor the grace of Jesus Christ in the gospel.

I grew up in a home where I knew I was loved, but my parents didn't seem to love each other. My dad was an alcoholic, and my older brother was an extremely angry child/teenager who became abusive to my mom and me. I didn't go to church or have any spiritual support to help me through this difficult time. So, I began to hate my brother. My feelings toward him escalated into ugly bitterness and heartache. I was thrilled when he was taken away to juvenile hall and later to prison. I felt safe then but also guilty and ashamed for my feelings.

At the age of 20, I thought I was in love and married a man that was also physically abusive. He drank and used drugs excessively. There were a few times in my marriage I thought I might lose my life if I didn't escape. Eventually, I decided to end this abusive marriage, and I moved home with my parents. In the darkest time of my life, I considered suicide. My mother, in her love for me, asked me to consider going to church. "You need God," she said, which caught me off guard. I didn't want to go to church, but I went, with feelings of hopelessness, shame, and loneliness.

On a Sunday morning in July of 1973, I heard the pastor talk about being freed from the guilt of bitterness and hatred. He said that there was hope for me through Christ and that I could be forgiven of all my sins. That was the best news I had ever heard. I could finally be free from the ugly feelings, the sins, I had been holding on to for years. I definitely wanted to be free. That morning, I trusted Him completely to change my life and make me a new person. He produced a hope in me that I couldn't explain, but I knew He was guiding me. He gave me peace and placed in my heart forgiveness for my brother and for the husband who had abused me. It was the best day of my life. I finally realized what Jesus had done for me on the cross—He took my bitterness, hatred, and guilt away. I have never been sorry for that wonderful, life-changing day 46 years ago.

The Word of God has been a light unto my path for over 40 years. After being saved at the age of 21, I went to a small Bible college in northern Indiana. I met my dear husband there, and in 1976, we began a life of ministry together. We gave our lives to working with teenagers at a large church in Pomona, California, in 1980. Then, in 1982, the Lord directed our hearts to restart a church in Hesperia, California. We served as pastor and wife at Mountain View Baptist Church for over 18 years. During our time there, I homeschooled my children for 13 years and have continued to this day to help in homeschooling my grandchildren.

In the fall of 2000, the Lord called my husband to plant churches in Utah and to encourage the pastors and missionaries already serving in Utah Valley. After being in Utah for only one year, my husband was diagnosed with pancreatic cancer, and six months later, he went home to be with the Lord. Walking through the valley of the shadow of death was one of the hardest times we as a family have ever experienced. Not only did I lose my husband, pastor, and best friend, but my children lost their father as well. He was only 49 years old when he left this world for his precious home in heaven. A few years later, the Lord brought a godly man into my life and the lives of my children. We fell in love and were married on May 28, 2005. Together, we have served in leadership and teaching positions to this day.

Teaching biblical truths has been the joy of my heart throughout my Christian life. I have led many ladies' Bible studies through the years, including a Bible study for women in the House of Hope Drug Rehab Center for over six years. By teaching an adult women's Sunday school and Bible study classes, I have had the privilege of helping women through the trials of life.

I see this book as an encouragement to anyone who will read it, but mostly to women who have been hurt, discouraged, abused, or depressed. It is my prayer that as you walk through the pages of this devotional, you will be inspired to love Christ, and to increase your faith in God and what He has done for you.

Dianna Moffitt Carroll

1

THERE'S ENCOURAGEMENT IN CHRIST

Philippians 2:1-4 ESV

So if there is any encouragement in Christ, any comfort from love, any participation in the Spirit, any affection and sympathy, complete my joy by being of the same mind, having the same love, being in full accord and of one mind. Do nothing from selfish ambition or conceit, but in humility count others more significant than yourselves. Let each of you look not only to his own interests, but also to the interests of others.

The small book of Philippians overflows with reassuring words such as: rejoicing, thanksgiving, and contentment. Paul is encouraging the church in Philippi to love all believers compassionately and affectionately as Christ has shown with all humility. His heart desires that all believers experience true joy, fellowship, and love for one another, esteeming one another in the compassion and mercy of Christ.

When Paul wrote, *"if there is any encouragement in Christ,"* he was saying if there is any help, counsel, or coming alongside to be someone's helper, then do this. It is interesting to note that Paul was in prison and caring for the interests of others as he penned these inspiring words. God has extended His great affection and mercy to every believer, which in the end should result in oneness in Christ. Divisiveness, and discord among the brethren are usually generated by only a few people in the church. Selfishness can consume a believer; and in the end, it can lead to a life of destruction. This kind of life breeds anger, resentment, and jealousy and is often clothed in self-righteousness, promoting one's spiritual abilities.

My Christian friend, encourage unity, and oneness among other believers. Put aside differences that produce strife, conflict, division, and opposition. Is your agenda first place in your life or are the needs of others more important? Are you esteeming others before yourself? True unity comes from a heart that cares for others more than caring for oneself. Christ established His church to motivate unity among believers that they may experience His wonderful joy.

Lord, may I put others before myself, showing mercy and affectionate compassion.

SURVIVING TROUBLES

Philippians 4:6-7 KJV

Be careful for nothing; but in every thing by prayer and supplication with thanksgiving let your requests be made known unto God. And the peace of God, which passeth all understanding, shall keep your hearts and minds through Christ Jesus.

Everyone has problems, but the question is, how do you deal with your problems? Do you break down or fall apart when things happen to you that you don't understand? Do you get angry or pout inwardly when hard times come? Have drugs, alcohol, overeating, or other things been your way of escape?

There are people who have a difficult time coping with the perplexities of life. To them, life is just existing or filled with too many challenges. Some of these dear people are extremely miserable, and they dislike their families, their spouses, their jobs, or even themselves. They live unhappy lives and to them it seems that nothing ever changes.

The biblical answer is that it is God who is at work in you to do His will for His good pleasure (Philippians 2:13). The apostle Paul learned the secret of surviving trouble. He was so secure in knowing that God was in control, he could sing in jail and stand boldly before the Greeks on Mars Hill, declaring his faith without hesitation. Paul stood fearlessly in the confidence of God before Felix, Festus, and Agrippa with his life in their hands.

Paul taught that you are to pray about everything and specifically with a thankful heart. When any burden arises, you are to ease your mind by praying and seeking wisdom and direction to lead you through the trial. Prayer is making not only your desires known before God but also your hurts. Prayer will help to keep you from sinning during your trials and from sinking under the load of them. Peace is a calming effect, without confusion or anxiety, and brings satisfaction to your soul. *"Thou wilt keep him in perfect peace, whose mind is stayed on thee"* (Isaiah 26:3).

Lord, thank You for prayer that brings perfect peace to my troubled heart.

(3)

DEPRESSION: IS IT SIN?

2 Corinthians 12:9 ESV

Is depression sin? Are there reasons for depression that we aren't aware of, and yet we believe it's sin? Can we move past the unfortunate situations in our lives that cause depression or are they out of our control? Job suffered circumstances that overwhelmed him and physically impaired him. Was he in sin? If someone suffers from a health issue that is debilitating and becomes depressed due to medication, is that person in sin? Do we try to understand what a person is going through and with love and compassion walk with him in his path of depression and pain?

If a person that is suffering from depression is a Christian, we may find Galatians 6:2 an important Scripture to read and obey: *"Bear one another's burdens . . ."* The death of a loved one or illnesses that are irreversible can cause depression. Accidents leaving a person disabled can cause a person to become depressed. Some people don't recognize their depression because they've blocked it out of their mind. Why? People have been taught that depression is a sin. But not all depression is caused by unconfessed sin. Most depression is from physical or emotional atrocities which have had devastating effects.

Sometimes, we believe that Christians are free from all despairing situations, but this is not true. We are fallen men and women, and sometimes we simply struggle with life. We live in sin-scarred bodies and in a sin-cursed world. Depression is not caused solely by our sinning, but because of life itself. If a person has not dealt with his sin, he can suffer from depression. But, it is damaging to say that all people suffering from depression are in sin. The apostle Paul said, *"We despaired of life itself"* (2 Corinthians 1:8). In 2 Corinthians 12:9, Christ said, *"My grace is sufficient for you, for **my power** is made perfect in weakness."* Paul's reply, *"Therefore I will boast all the more gladly of my weaknesses, so that the **power of Christ** may rest upon me."*

Lord, may I have compassion on those who are in depression.

4

I AM NOTHING WITHOUT LOVE

1 Corinthians 13

We need to ask ourselves this question: Are we loving? That could be a hard question to answer. Maybe we should ask: Are we patient? Are we kind? Are we trusting? These types of questions are more a matter of the heart. Can we measure ourselves according to these qualities of love? The Word of God says, "If we don't have love, we are nothing."

Jesus said in John 13:35, *"By this shall all men know that ye are my disciples, if ye have love one to another."* Making the choice to love others is a command given by our Lord to those who would call themselves Christians.

Abraham Lincoln made a lot of friends, and he also made some enemies during our great Civil War. Edwin Stanton, Secretary of War during President Lincoln's administration, was said to be rude, explosive, dogmatic, and obstinate. Yet Lincoln chose him for that particular job.

History teaches us that although Stanton was rude and abrasive, he couldn't resist the patience that Lincoln showed him. Stanton could not resist the non-retaliating spirit of Lincoln. Love forgives seventy times seven when it has been wronged. Long-suffering endures the insults and injuries of others, and kindness pays them back only with deeds of goodness and unfeigned love.

On the night of Lincoln's assassination, Stanton stood in the little room where the President's body was taken. Peering down into the silent face of the President in all its ruggedness, he reportedly uttered this famous remark: "Now he belongs to the ages." Stanton knew the kind of man President Lincoln was and appreciated the kind-hearted spirit he shared with those who served with him.

The Bible never defines love but describes it. Love is an action word, and love is only love when it acts. The true Christian is one who loves when he is hurt, wounded, or taken advantage of without seeking revenge.

Lord, may I learn to share my love by what I do and not only by what I say.

5

CONDITIONAL OR GRACE?

Ephesians 2:1-10 ESV

"For by grace you have been saved. . ."

Have you ever felt that most of your relationships were overlaid with conditions? If you love me, then I will love you. If you give to me, then I will give to you. When you serve me, then I will serve you. Will you ever find the right conditions to meet the other person's needs and secure your happiness? Must you always do something for someone in order for him to accept you? Is the underlying message always that accomplishments and performance precede approval?

Everyone knows what it's like not to measure up to someone's expectations. This oppressive conditionality is quite real in our society today and exhausting to live under. We see conditions, prerequisites, and requirements placed upon not only people in the world but also many Christians.

What about grace? Grace is the outpouring of love that seeks you out when you have absolutely nothing to give in return. This love is not about preconditions that require accomplishments and approval. It is about being loved when you are undeserving of that love, a gift of God's grace, pure and simple.

The relationship where you continuously feel like you're being evaluated and falling short of someone's acceptance is an unhappy relationship. The gospel liberates you from the judgment of God and of mankind. You'll never measure up to the demands that are placed upon you; therefore, you are in need of a Savior.

It is an unconditional love that relieves the pressure of demands, forgives all our failures, and replaces our unrelenting fears with faith. Jesus Christ came to set us free from the tireless effort of justifying ourselves and finding approval in the eyes of men. The Bible is saturated with the message of grace and the love that God lavishes upon us. Even though we may try to insist on paying our sin debt, the balance has been settled, paid in full, by His grace!

Lord, thank You for Your unconditional love.

LIFE'S DISAPPOINTMENTS

1 Samuel 22:1-5; 2 Samuel 22:51

David, the anointed king, is running from King Saul's attempts to kill him and hides in the cave of Adullam. His brethren and all his father's house hear of his plight and come to the cave to join David. All who were distressed, in debt, and discontented congregated in the cave with David. Would you, being in the situation that David was in, discouraged and fearful for his life, want a crowd of disgruntled, frustrated, irritated, restless, annoyed, and broken people in your cave? Four hundred men take up a great deal of space; and given their circumstances, they could be quite discouraging to have around.

Can God take the most troublesome circumstances and turn them for your good? Were the years David spent battling hardship and disappointment all in vain or did God take these trials and turn them into tremendous times of growth and preparation for what God had in store for him?

What is it that will bring you to the point of disappointment and discouragement in your life? Will you turn away from God or will you let Him embrace you with His wondrous love and mercy? If you can identify the source of discouragement and trust in Christ, you will find *"rest unto your souls"* (Matthew 11:28-29).

Satan wants us to focus on areas of weakness in our lives, such as gossip, unforgiveness, anger, and bitterness. We can't think clearly when we're focused on the lies of Satan. His lies divide our minds and cause us to blame God and others. If we continue to live in this harmful condition, we will eventually suffer the consequences. Our understanding of Scripture is essential.

How do we emerge from our disappointment and find contentment? We must realize that God is aware of our circumstances and nothing catches Him off guard. The various testings of our faith will produce steadfastness in our lives (James 1:2-4).

Lord, thank You for Your Word that encourages my weary soul.

7

WHEN LIFE HURTS

2 Corinthians 12:9 ESV

But he said to me, "My grace is sufficient for you, for my power is made perfect in weakness." Therefore I will boast all the more gladly of my weaknesses, so that the power of Christ may rest upon me.

Have you ever hurt so badly that you felt like your heart would burst inside? Did you feel like the pain you were experiencing was overwhelming and there seemed to be no end in sight? A Christian's life is not excluded from perplexing circumstances that are uncomfortable or even painful. If you read the story of Paul, you will see that the events of his life were filled with distressing and traumatic trials.

Without experiencing the agonizing days of being shipwrecked, beaten, stoned, and afflicted with a thorn in the flesh (2 Corinthians 11:24-28; 12:7-8), how could he ever write, *"My grace is sufficient for you"*? Paul realized that the power to fully endure such adverse situations came only through the power of God. How else could he rejoice in prison and be able to sing praises to God in the midst of such hostile and unfavorable times?

You too have God's unsearchable grace that enables you to endure life when it hurts so badly. His *"grace is sufficient for you"* means His grace is enough, and it is necessary to be able to go through the hard times of life. His grace enables you to forgive those who have wounded you beyond what you thought you could ever endure. And His grace gives you the assurance that *"all things work together for good to them that love God"* (Romans 8:28). Knowing that His grace is "sufficient" is essential in the life of a Christian. When you realize that God's divine grace is one of His richest attributes, then His power to endure rests upon you. Paul wrote that he could have the strength to withstand all things *"through Him who strengthens me"* (Philippians 4:13).

Lord, through You I know I can endure all things, even when life hurts so badly.

8

I'M TROUBLED, BUT NOT IN DESPAIR

Psalm 143:4, 8, 10 NASB

Therefore my spirit is overwhelmed within me; My heart is appalled within me. . . . Let me hear Your lovingkindness in the morning; For I trust in You; Teach me the way in which I should walk; For to You I lift up my soul. . . . Teach me to do Your will, For You are my God.

David was seeking God for deliverance in a time of great trial. It is a refuge for us to know that we are guarded on every side through God's faithfulness and that He will guide us through our times of trouble. Sometimes our feelings get in the way and we are "overwhelmed" within. David wrote, *"Why are you cast down, O my soul, and why are you in turmoil within me?"* (Psalm 42:11). Our feelings can sometimes govern our ability to think right, and we lose sight of what God is doing in and through us.

David asked for forgiveness and was seeking God's mercy

and deliverance from his many enemies. With troubled feelings, he pleaded for the light of God's countenance to shine upon him and for God to give him wisdom and understanding. As Christians, we too should be seeking God, asking for His mercy to deliver us from those whose aim is to hurt and ruin us. In the New Testament, Paul wrote, *"We are troubled on every side, yet not distressed; we are perplexed, but not in despair"* (2 Corinthians 4:8). Paul, like David, was showing that in the conflict of soul and endless suffering, he was not crippled or cast down, but strengthened through Christ (2 Corinthians 12:9).

Maybe, it's not an enemy that seeks to cause pain, but a friend or a loved one that has brought despair and heartache. This can cause tremendous suffering, agony, and torment to the soul. Ask God to teach you how you should walk through this time of distress, and trust Him to do His will in you.

Lord, I trust You with my troubled soul.

SUFFERING FOR HIS SAKE

Philippians 1:27, 29 NASB

Only conduct yourselves in a manner worthy of the gospel of Christ, so that whether I come and see you or remain absent, I will hear of you that you are standing firm in one spirit, with one mind striving together for the faith of the gospel. . . . For to you it has been granted for Christ's sake, not only to believe in Him, but also to suffer for His sake.

Paul, a citizen of heaven, wants the Philippian church to realize that the world around them can only see the true gospel by what they view in their lives. We are to conduct ourselves in a manner worthy of the gospel of Christ. The most powerful weapon against the enemy of Christ is the consistent life of a believer living out the gospel day after day.

The sufferings of the Philippian Christians were mentioned more than once by Paul in his writings. If we suffer for

Christ's sake, we are to consider it a precious gift from Him (Matthew 5:11-12). We are to labor together for the gospel's sake and not against one another. We are to be of one spirit and one mind, standing against any opposition of the gospel Satan may bring .

Paul tells believers that when they stand for the sake of the gospel, they will suffer persecution. He instructs them to be consistent in living their lives worthy of the gospel; and in the end, they will receive a great reward. *"If we suffer, we shall also reign with him: if we deny him, he also will deny us"* (2 Timothy 2:12, KJV). Paul informs the people that there is an enemy that wants to steal this treasure from them and cripple the ministry of the gospel; but God gives the grace we need to go through any trial and enables us to have joy in the midst of every battle.

Lord, may I ever walk worthy of the gospel of Christ, though trials may disrupt my path and obscure my way.

A TROUBLED HEART

Psalm 38:6 KJV

I am troubled; I am bowed down greatly; I go mourning all the day long.

As Christians, we can quickly find ourselves with a troubled heart. We are troubled with sin from within and burdened by foes without. We are on a path that is difficult, and we become weary on our journey. When we seek comfort from those around us, we find sorrow. When we expect help, we find hindrances and discouragement. We thought life promised pleasures, but instead we found pain and difficulties with a reluctant heart to move forward.

The sin is too heavy to bear, and we've allowed wrong thoughts to invade our minds. Giving in to the trial becomes an option we'd consider. What do we do and to whom do we turn to find the relief we so desperately need? There is mercy and grace for us in our pain and despair, knowing our

Lord experienced such sorrow of heart. In His darkest hour, Jesus spoke these words to His disciples in the garden of Gethsemane, "*My soul is exceeding sorrowful, even unto death*" (Matthew 26:38, KJV).

In the midst of a troubled heart, we can become completely overwhelmed and feel utterly devastated. But, if our hearts are focused on Christ and not on the things of this world, the promises of God are already secure. In this light and momentary trouble, He is preparing for us an eternal weight of glory beyond all comparison. The sufferings we are enduring at this present time are not equal to the glory that is to be revealed to us in heaven. Why do we worry and have a troubled heart? We need to fix our hearts and minds on Him, the Author and Finisher of our faith, who is preparing for us a home of abundant glory.

Lord, may I direct my heart toward the things above in anticipation of my home in glory.

FACING TEMPTATION

1 Corinthians 10:13 KJV

There hath no temptation taken you but such as is common to man: but God is faithful, who will not suffer you to be tempted above that ye are able.

Rejecting a bad habit requires changing one's lifestyle and making no provision for the flesh (Romans 13:14). Biblical transformation takes place through the power of the Holy Spirit working in our lives. For instance, the person who wants to stop smoking should throw away all his cigarettes and not buy any more. The person battling with substance abuse should avoid the company of those who have the same problem (1 Corinthians 15:33). They should avoid the places and circumstances which they know will tempt them.

Those wrestling with a sinful habit need to understand that there is a difference between temptation and sin. When you choose to pursue the temptation, that's when it becomes sin.

To be tempted isn't sin, for even our Lord was tempted. The deciding factor is how will you respond to the temptation? Will you pursue wrong thoughts and let them materialize in your mind? So many Christians think that victory over sin means that they will no longer be tempted. The temptation is not a sin; it is a preparation to fight. Since we will always be tempted, we need to understand that God is wise as well as faithful to help us through our temptation (1 Corinthians 10:13).

Take personal responsibility for your own sinful habits, but don't try to fight temptation alone. Find a mature Christian to help you through the hard times. They need to check up on you and encourage you to be honest with yourself and your failures. You must trust God and His faithfulness to give you a way of escape so that you will be able to endure such times when you are tempted. Preach the gospel to yourself daily, and give thanks for His righteousness which is accredited to your account through Christ alone.

Lord, help me to fight this sinful habit before me.

WHY DO WE SUFFER?

Job 1:1 KJV

There was a man in the land of Uz, whose name was Job; and that man was perfect and upright, and one that feared God, and eschewed evil.

In the opening of the book of Job, a scene is described in heaven where Job is accused of serving God because God protects him. Satan is seeking God's consent to test Job and is given permission to try him in his faith, within certain boundaries. The question, "Why do the righteous suffer?" was asked after Job lost all of his wealth, his family, and his health. The three so-called friends of Job came to "comfort" him but, instead, began to criticize him about his adversity. They repeatedly said that the suffering in his life was punishment for sin.

Nothing can be done to us by Satan unless God has given permission for him to do so. God has power over Satan, and we will never truly understand the "whys" of pain and suffering brought on by him. We must also realize that not all suffering is because of sin, or the way one lives, but because God wants to test, teach, or purify our lives through some kind of adversity. Scripture teaches us that God's grace is enough and will sustain us with strength in our weakness through any trial (2 Corinthians 12:9). He desires to produce in us what He deserves from us—our love, praise, and thanksgiving in every trying circumstance (1 Thessalonians 5:18).

Job makes us realize that there are situations going on in our lives that we usually know nothing about. God will allow things to capture our attention, but we commonly respond by questioning God's goodness without seeing the full picture. Job reminds us to trust God under all circumstances, especially when we do not understand what's happening. "As for God, His way is perfect" (Psalm 18:30). Because God's ways are "perfect," we can trust whatever He does—and whatever He allows—to also be perfect.

Lord, may I rely on Your grace and trust You through each trial.

BETRAYED

Psalm 41:9 NASB

Even my close friend in whom I trusted, who ate my bread, has lifted up his heel against me.

Throughout history, we have read and seen man betray man, brother betray brother and friend betray friend. One of the most heart-stirring occasions is that of the betrayal of Jesus for thirty pieces of silver by a man named Judas Iscariot.

Matthew 26:47-49 shows Judas coming with a great multitude of men carrying swords and strong wooden sticks to arrest Jesus in the garden. The sign of betrayal, a kiss, was placed on His cheek. The word *kiss* means "a touch with the lips as a sign of love or reverence." Was there love or reverence for our Lord at this time? Not so!

David, the son of Jesse anointed by Samuel to be king of Israel, was betrayed by King Saul. David and King Saul's son

Jonathan were friends, and it could be said that they were "of one mind" and loved one another. David was asked often to play the harp to soothe the heart of King Saul when his soul was troubled. David went to battle for King Saul and protected him from those that would take his life. David never lifted his hand against God's anointed, yet he was betrayed by him.

What do you do when those you call "friend" have lifted their heels against you? How do you act or react when this catastrophe occurs? Our Lord was troubled in spirit and soul with Judas' betrayal in the garden (Matthew 26:24). He knew who would betray Him yet lifted not His hand against him. This event gives us an example of how Christ would have us treat those who have betrayed us or will betray us. He did nothing. He willingly allowed Judas to betray Him, knowing this was the Father's will. In these painful situations, can you do nothing, knowing this is the Father's will for you?

Lord, I forgive those who have betrayed me as You forgave those who betrayed You while hanging on the cross.

WITHOUT FAITH

John 8:12-59

For most people, the Bible has become only an instruction manual on how to live the Christian life which is good and right. But, we should also see the Christ of the Bible as, *"the Light of life,"* the only way to salvation. We are in need of someone who will rescue us from our prison of sin, because we are unable to free ourselves from that sin debt. Luke 19:10 says, *"For the Son of Man came to seek and to save the lost."*

In John chapter 8, Jesus is teaching in the temple during the time of the Feast of Tabernacles (Booths) and begins to speak of Himself, saying, *"I am the Light of the World."* He is claiming to be the *"I AM"* from Exodus 3:13-15. Levitical law says to pick up a stone and kill him who claims to be equal with God (Leviticus 24:10-16). Jesus is connecting Himself to God the Father and tells them, *"Whoever follows me will not walk in darkness, but will have the Light of life"* (John 8:12).

John is focusing on faith and spiritual slavery and teaches whoever practices sin is in slavery to sin—the sin of unbelief. *"I told you that you would die in your sins, for unless you believe that I am he you will die in your sins"* (John 8:24). While Jesus accuses the Pharisees of being children of the devil (John 8:42-47), He tells them that the reason why they don't hear what He is saying is because they are not of God. The Pharisees could not bring themselves to faith by their own efforts. Believing the lies of Satan blinds us to the truth of the gospel (Ephesians 2:1-3). To obey the words of Christ in John 8 is to put one's faith in Christ. Our hope in salvation does not rest in our faithfulness but in His faithfulness alone. We are saved because Jesus saves us.

Lord, thank You for faith to believe.

15

BELIEVING BY FAITH

John 9

John's writings are straightforward in describing Jesus as deity. He was accused of breaking the Sabbath when He healed an invalid man after thirty-eight years of being bedridden. He called God His Father, making Himself equal with God. This infuriated the Jews and is why they were seeking to kill Him. In John 8, He calls Himself, "The Light of the World," and "before Abraham was, I AM." After hearing this, the crowd picked up stones to throw at Him, but He hid and left the temple because it was not yet His time.

In John 9, Jesus passed by a man born blind. His disciples asked Him, "Rabbi, who sinned, this man or his parents?" Jesus answered, "It was not that this man sinned, or his parents, but that the works of God might be displayed in him."

Because Jesus healed the man on the Sabbath, the Jews brought the man who was formerly blind to the Pharisees.The Jews didn't believe the man had been born blind, so they asked his parents. The parents were fearful to speak and said, "He is of age, you ask him about his blindness." The parents didn't want to be put out of the synagogue by the Jews, for the Jews had already decided that if anyone confessed Jesus to be the Christ they would not be allowed in the synagogue. The Jews reviled (angrily criticized) the man that once was blind and cast him out of the assembly.

After Jesus heard that they had cast him out, He found the man and asked him, "Do you believe in the Son of Man?" After finding out who Jesus was, the man said, "Lord, I believe," and he worshiped him. Jesus will die on the cross after using the phrase "Son of Man" over 80 times; and notably, He used it more than any other title. The proclamation by Jesus that He was the "Son of Man" holds great value in saying, *"He is the One given everlasting dominion, which shall not pass away, or be destroyed"* (Daniel 7:13-14).

Lord, by faith, I believe.

TRUSTING GOD TO BE ENOUGH

Psalms 73:28 KJV

*But it is good for me to draw near to God: I have put my **trust** in the Lord GOD, that I may declare all thy works.*

There are times in our lives when our hearts are broken, and we don't know what to do. We try to trust God, but it's difficult and our circumstances are severely discouraging. We begin to fall into the pit of despair and can't seem to find our way out. In the dreadful pit, we allow our imagination to run wild; and in the darkness of pain, we begin to imagine that God is not there.

Our minds begin to assume that God is not all that He says that He is or that He will not do what He has promised. We sometimes reason against the knowledge of God and without the light of the gospel, we become dull of hearing. Can a person really trust God? Is He dependable and faithful? Does His endless love actually surround a person who trusts in Him? Psalms 32:10 says, *"Many sorrows shall be to the wicked: but he that trusteth in the LORD, mercy shall compass him about."*

It isn't easy to trust God, especially during times of pain and adversity. Nobody enjoys suffering; and when it comes, we want to be relieved as quickly as possible. Do you have a relationship with God that exhibits confidence in His care for you? Or, in your intense sorrow, have you been blinded by grief and see no evidence of God at all? Are God and His Word enough in your burden of affliction to restore your trust in Him or has your imagination taken you to the point of doubt and distrust?

As bleak as life may seem for you, God's lovingkindness is always present, and His incredible constancy endures forever. May we never forget God's goodness, forgiveness, and compassion toward us. Hurting friend, trust that God is enough, and know He never changes!

Lord, I am trusting that You are enough.

LIFE WHEN IT HURTS

Galatians 6:2 ESV

Bear one another's burdens, and so fulfill the law of Christ.

What does it mean to fulfill the law of Christ? Most Bible teachers say that the law of Christ is what Jesus stated in Mark 12:29-31, *"Love the Lord your God with all your heart . . . soul . . . mind and . . . strength.' . . . 'love your neighbor as yourself.' There is no other commandment greater than these."*

Are there things that you wish others knew and could understand when life brings real heart-wrenching pain and your grief overpowers every dream you hold dear? Sometimes people with good intentions say foolish and harmful things to those suffering. Instead of giving hope and strength in an ongoing crisis, they can wound an already broken heart to the point of devastation.

Someone in sorrow needs you to come alongside and give him encouragement through a touch of compassion and a tearful, tender heart (Romans 12:15). Even though the question, "How are you doing?" seems like the right thing to ask, it can seem to the wounded and distressed that they need to give a report of their actions, thoughts, or emotions. There's no time limit on grieving, and people from all walks of life suffer differently.

Expressing an impatient attitude toward a hurting person is jarring to the senses. It can cause despondency, the loss of hope; and despair, the feeling that no favorable outcome will ever exist. Be thoughtful in quoting Scripture such as Romans 8:28; most likely, things are not good for that person right now, nor does it seem like there will ever be anything positive come out of his circumstances.

Helping someone who is in deep sorrow to recognize the sovereignty of God is what he needs most. Knowing that He is in absolute authority over all things brings peace and reminds him to "be still" and rest in the knowledge that God is always his Refuge and Comforter (Psalms 46:10; 91:1-2; John 14:16).

Lord, may I fulfill the law of Christ, bearing another's burden.

(18)

OUR HIGHEST FOCUS

Ecclesiastes 12:13 NASB

Fear God and keep his commandments, because this applies to every person.

Is there true satisfaction in the things of this world? Are some of man's greatest and most notable achievements only efforts ending in emptiness and pride? It has been incredible what man has accomplished, yet God is rarely given the acknowledgment due His name. The theme and purpose of the book of Ecclesiastes are revealed through the reflections and experiences of just one man, King Solomon. He was the wisest man that ever lived and declared he had seen everything *"under the sun"* (Ecclesiastes 1:14). In his conclusion to the whole matter, Solomon determined that man's existence was filled with futility and hopelessness. In his pursuit of the real meaning of human life, all that he had sought after was meaningless.

The apostle Paul wrote about all he had accomplished religiously before he was confronted by Christ on the road to Damascus (Philippians 3:4-6). His conclusion, *"For his sake I have suffered the loss of all things and count them as rubbish, in order that I may gain Christ"* (Philippians 3:8). Paul's greatest desire was to *"know him and the power of his resurrection, and the fellowship of his sufferings, being conformed to his death"* (Philippians 3:10).

Our purpose in life is to glorify God and enjoy fellowship with Him. Because of the fall of man, fellowship with God has been broken and man struggles to find peace and joy. Only through faith in Jesus Christ can purpose in life be discovered. To exalt God is to fear and obey Him while keeping our hearts fixed on our future home, heaven. His purpose for our lives enables us to experience true and lasting joy———the abundant life He desires for every believer. *"The thief comes only to steal and kill and destroy. I came that they may have life and have it abundantly"* (John 10:10).

Lord, may my greatest achievement in life be to trust You and love You with all my heart.

DON'T VIOLATE YOUR CONSCIENCE

Acts 24:16 NASB

In view of this, I also do my best to maintain always a blameless conscience both before God and before men.

Have you taken great pains to have a clean conscience before God and man, or have you allowed the world to instruct you to ignore your guilt feelings and make your conscience weak? This is a dangerous way to live your life as a Christian.

God has graciously given you something within that is powerful to assist you in the struggle against sin. He gave you a conscience, and that conscience can bring you real pleasure and freedom. Examining your guilt feelings in the light of Scripture and then confessing and forsaking your sin will cleanse your conscience. Dealing with sin immediately is a continuous quality or aspect of the

Christian life. It is a privilege and joy to walk before God with a clear conscience.

Sometimes people think their guilty conscience will just clear up over time without dealing with it. But guilty feelings can remain for long periods of time and appear in other areas of life, causing one to feel guilty and not know the reason for it. This could be a sign that something is definitely wrong spiritually (Titus 1:15). A weak conscience that is easily grieved is a result of a lack of knowledge and understanding of the Word of God. You need to respond to your conscience, even if it's weak, and continue to learn from God's Word. It would be wise to never ignore your conscience or live by your feelings alone (Jeremiah 17:9). The Spirit of God helps us in our weaknesses, our infirmities, and searches the heart of man (Romans 8:26-27).

What is your conscience trying to say to you? Can you respond with Paul in saying, "*I have lived in all good conscience before God until this day*" (Acts 23:1)? Christians need to fight to keep a pure and good conscience every day.

Lord, may I keep a clear conscience that is right before You and others.

(20)

GIVE ME LIVING WATER

John 4:9-10 ESV

"How is it that you, a Jew, ask for a drink from me, a woman of Samaria?" . . . Jesus answered her, "If you knew the gift of God, and who it is that is saying to you, 'Give me a drink,' you would have asked him, and he would have given you living water."

The narrative of the Samaritan woman at the well of Sychar is an extremely touching story and one filled with Jesus' humanity as well as His divine power to save sinners. Scripture says Jesus was wearied from His journey and sat down at the well around the sixth hour (John 4:6). The sixth hour would be sometime around noon and the hottest part of the day. The women of the city did not come to fill their water pots at this time but came earlier in the day or later in the evening when it was cooler.

This woman was not only a Samaritan but a woman with a soiled and shameful reputation as well. It could be said that

Jesus had a heavenly appointment with this woman. He was there to share with her the true and living water, not from a well but from God Himself, the Redeemer of her soul. She was inquisitive of not only His motive for wanting water from her but also why He would risk His reputation and talk to her in public. Jewish men did not talk to women in public; it was taboo.

God, in the flesh, was sitting at the well, offering the Samaritan woman "living water." An allusion from Jeremiah in the Old Testament metaphorically refers to the Jews forsaking God and His grace and missing the cleansing power through the Spirit of God (Jeremiah 2:1-13). *"They have forsaken me, the fountain of living waters, and hewed out cisterns for themselves, broken cisterns that can hold no water" (v. 13).* The children of Israel were trusting earthly, broken-down cisterns for their physical water. They were also relying on themselves, and not on the true and living God.

Lord, thank You for living water.

21

IS THERE HOPE AT THE WELL?

John 4:13-14 NASB

Jesus answered and said to her, "Everyone who drinks of this water will thirst again; but whoever drinks of the water that I will give him shall never thirst; but the water that I will give him will become in him a well of water springing up to eternal life."

Addictions are relentless, whether they are substance abuse, sexual obsessions, food cravings, or perfectionism. God created us with two basic parts: the physical person, which we can see, and the inner person, which only God can see. The inner, spiritual part is the heart, soul, spirit, and mind of a person and is responsible before God for the choices made in the flesh. The term *addiction* means "to devote or surrender (oneself) to something habitually or obsessively." That something could be just about anything———including the sin you're struggling with at this moment.

Lust is a biblical term that is likened to an unquenchable thirst. You will never be fulfilled by pursuing the lust of the flesh, because lust is Satan's lie. He will promise you happiness, love, and peace, but has he succeeded? No! No matter how many new things you try or search after, nothing will EVER bring you true satisfaction or fill your heart with joy. Only Christ can create real contentment and replenish your thirsty soul with living water.

Perhaps you've been deceived and have found yourself doing things you thought you'd never do. Are you desiring love and acceptance? Are you expecting sexual sin to satisfy you when it's like drinking water out of a sewer and imagining it's pure spring water? Jesus compared physical thirst with the Samaritan woman's attempts to quench the thirst of her soul with multiple sinful relationships. Jesus offered her *"living water,"* which would quench her thirst once and for all. Please turn to Jesus to rid your life of any sinful behaviors and waters that do not satisfy..

Lord, I desire Your living water to satisfy and restore my thirsty soul.

22

WHY ARE YOU SO FEARFUL?

Mark 4:35-41 KJV

And he said unto them, Why are ye so fearful? how is it that ye have no faith? And they feared exceedingly, and said one to another, What manner of man is this, that even the wind and the sea obey him?

Jesus was preaching before a large crowd but needed space between Himself and the crowd of people surrounding Him. He stepped into a boat and pushed off into the water a little, giving Himself room. Christ, being exhausted by all He had done that day, went to the other side of the Sea of Galilee to rest. While Jesus was asleep in the stern of the boat, a fierce storm arose, filling the boat with water. The disciples, being afraid, awoke Him and said to Him, "Master, do You not care that we are perishing? How can you sleep when we are going through this?" They panicked. The disciples knew Jesus had power over the natural world as well as the supernatural world, but they questioned His ability to save them from the storm.

Jesus got up and rebuked the wind and the sea, saying, "Peace, be still." The wind died down, and it became perfectly calm. He said to the men, "Why are you so fearful? How is it that ye have no faith?" Immediately, they became "exceedingly fearful" and said to one another, "What manner of man is this, that even the wind and the sea obey him?"

Why are we afraid of the storms of life when the Creator of this world lives within us? How can we be fearful of any circumstance when Christ, the Author and Finisher of our faith, dwells in our mortal bodies? The strong winds of fear may invade our anxious minds, but when Christ, the Creator and Captain of the sea, speaks, may we surrender full command of the storm to the One who can calm the raging sea and bring PEACE to our troubled soul.

Lord, I surrender full command of the storm in my life to You.

23

LIVING BY FAITH OR IN FEAR?

1 Corinthians 2:5 ESV

That your faith might not rest [stand] in the wisdom of men but in the power of God.

Does fear take hold of your emotions in your day-to-day life? Is it possible to develop a faith that conquers all your fears? Do you understand that faith comes from God and is not something you can produce in and of yourself?

In Psalm 56:3, David reveals his faith with these words: *"When I am afraid, I will put my trust in you."* Psalm 119 is filled with verses expressing the way in which David treasured God's Word: *"With my whole heart I seek you"* (v. 10); *"I will meditate on your precepts"* (v. 15); *"I have stored up your word in my heart"* (v. 11). What wisdom those words speak to us today. It's not in David we put our trust but in the power of the gospel, the finished work of Christ.

Though in Christ we are more than conquerors (Romans

8:37), on occasion, we allow intimidating circumstances to distract us from the truth of the Word of God. When we focus on our fears, overwhelming feelings of helplessness rob us of the joy there is in Christ alone. *"The LORD is on my side; I will not fear"* (Psalm 118:6).

God is gracious and understanding toward our weaknesses. But the Bible is clear that our faith does not mature and strengthen us without trials. When we face unbearable circumstances, remember that Romans 5:3 says, *"Suffering produces endurance."* If someone turns against us, we can be comforted by the words in Romans 8:31, *"If God is for us, who can be against us?"* Throughout life, we will continue to face various trials that would cause us fear. According to His Word, God assures us that we can know a peace through every situation, *"the peace of God, which surpasses all understanding,"* which He has promised will *"guard your hearts and your minds in Christ Jesus"* (Philippians 4:7).

Lord, when I'm afraid, I will trust in You.

24

HAVE YOU LIED TO YOURSELF?

Matthew 7:1-5 KJV

Hypocrite, first cast out the beam out of thine own eye.

It's not easy coming to terms with your sinfulness. Seeing the beam in your own eye is like coming out of a bad movie and realizing that you were the featured actor/actress. Your part, judging and condemning people. Oh, the pride, in all of its corruption, protrudes from the realization that **you** are guilty of being negative, disapproving, and judgmental. You have been blinded to your own sin, yet others could not help but see who you really are. The lie you told yourself is finally played out, and the truth emerges. You ultimately see the critical, fault-finding spirit that lives in your heart.

When our well-kept secret is finally uncovered, things begin to crumble. Because our foundation has been resting upon a rotten core, the support of a previous arrogance and confidence will crack and then collapse. The safe covering we enjoyed behind our sin is gone. The more we convince ourselves that we're better than most, the more painful the revealing becomes. Who we are is now in plain view for all to see, and we must be wholly dependent on His grace.

As we arrive at this level of conviction, we can no longer pretend or make-believe. We thought our sin would never come out, but it did. We have been acting like this for years, and it has become a practice that seems impossible to stop. Are we under some illusion that through mere methods we have the power to change our path from sin to righteousness? True repentance brings our sin to the throne of grace where real transformation takes place.

Psalm 51:1-10 says in part, "*Have mercy upon me, O God,. . . blot out my transgressions. Wash me thoroughly from mine iniquity,. . . my sin is ever before me. Against thee, thee only, have I sinned. . . . Create in me a clean heart, O God; and renew a right spirit within me.*"

Lord, I have sinned against You, and I repent!

$$25$$

LEARNING THROUGH LOSS, SUFFERING, AND DEATH

Job 1:21, 22 KJV

Naked came I out of my mother's womb, and naked shall I return thither: the LORD gave, and the LORD hath taken away; blessed be the name of the LORD. In all this Job sinned not, nor charged God foolishly.

There once lived a man from the land of Uz whose name has become synonymous with words like suffering, loss, and death. This man's name was Job. All ten of his children were taken in death, his herds amounting to thousands were destroyed, and his good health was taken from him. How did Job respond to loss? Was he bitter, angry, or cynical? Job's reaction to hardship and pain was forever recorded in Scripture. There are few people that can handle loss with such maturity as Job. He was described as a man who was perfect, upright, and one who feared God and shunned evil. According to God, there was no man on earth quite like Job (Job 2:3).

Can a Christian face a variety of impossible circumstances and still find God to be good? Joseph was sold into slavery, yet God meant it for good. David suffered from the hands of King Saul, running for his life, yet God protected him. Paul was stoned, shipwrecked, and imprisoned, yet God loved him and gave him sustaining grace.

If a Christian cannot submit to the superior wisdom of God and His purpose for pain, then he or she will never see suffering as a privilege. When our world turns upside down and all that we see seems hideous to our finite minds, that's when we have an opportunity to submit our wills to His supreme authority. Job was a man who suffered tremendous loss; yet through his tragic heartache, he spoke these compelling words, *"Though he slay me, yet will I trust in him"* (Job 13:15.) Every child of God must travel with his Lord across some stormy seas, knowing that this experience is a high calling of God (1 Peter 4:19).

Lord, through every difficult circumstance, may I trust Your sufficient grace in suffering.

26

IN THE STORMS OF LIFE, WILL YOUR ANCHOR HOLD?

Hebrews 6:17-20 KJV

Which hope we have as an anchor of the soul, both sure and stedfast.

What storms in life are you dealing with at this moment? Are you in the storm of life-threatening health issues and nothing seems to be going the way you thought it would? Are you in the storm of a marriage relationship so rocky it could come to the point of shipwreck (divorce)? Are you in the storm of overwhelming financial loss and there's no visible hope that you will see relief tomorrow? Has a child that you have loved and nurtured in the ways of the Lord left the faith he was rooted in?

How do you find peace in these storms and know that Jesus will never let you go? How do you turn painful memories into blessings and build a solid foundation of faith and trust? How do you receive daily strength and encouragement, turning every agonizing heartache into experiencing God's secure protection? Have you asked yourself these questions and many more like them?

I want to encourage your heart with a powerful thought for surviving daily struggles and temptations in the difficulties of life. No case is too hard for God and no problem is too difficult to overcome when we *hope* in God and replace fear and doubt with peace (John 14:27). We must realize that a ship that is anchored will not be prevented from being hurled about nor will those on board escape from becoming seasick. Though we may be tossed around, we are safe, for we have an anchor of the soul that is both secure and faithful. Just as we prepare for a ravaging storm by anchoring valuables to a solid foundation, we are to anchor our hearts in the firm foundation of faith to help us withstand the testing and trials of life that are certain to come our way.

Lord, help us not to resent the storms of life that come or be fearful of their effects.

27

FROM SLAVERY TO FREEDOM TO BONDSERVANT

1 Corinthians 7:22 NASB

For he who was called in the Lord while a slave, is the Lord's freedman; likewise he who was called while free, is Christ's slave.

There have been many forms of slavery written about in our history books, including the enslavement of people recorded in Scripture. The Bible does not condemn slavery altogether since the Bible gives instructions on how to treat a slave or bondservant (Colossians 4:1). During Bible times, slavery was sometimes pursued to aid and assist people struggling to stay alive. They would sell themselves to provide for their families or to get out of debt.

We suffered a great Civil War here in our country because of the unfavorable practice of slavery. This harmful action was directed toward the color of a person's skin rather than his specific need for economic assistance. Men, women, and children were unlawfully taken from their homes and forced to become slaves. They were treated as inferior human beings and abused physically and mentally. Freedom from this type of slavery was costly, and many family members fought against each other during this difficult time. Roughly 2% of the population, an estimated 620,000 men, lost their lives in this devastating war.

The Word of God does tell us that we are born in sin and therefore slaves to sin (Psalm 51:5; Romans 6:16-20). But, when we trust Christ by faith and believe in what He has done for us through His death, burial, and resurrection, we are freed from the bondage of sin and its condemnation (Romans 8:1-2). When a person becomes a servant to Christ through regeneration, the Bible says he is then a slave, bound to serve but free to express his deep devotion to Christ. How can one not express such gratitude and overwhelming love for Him. Once slaves to sin, but now, children of God, and heirs of God through Jesus Christ our Lord (Galatians 4:7).

Lord, thank You for the freedom to serve and to be Your servant.

28

LIVING BY OUR EMOTIONS

2 Corinthians 5:7 ESV

For we walk by faith, not by sight.

The Lord gives us a wonderful example of how to cope with human feelings. Jesus Christ, as fully man and fully God, experienced all human emotions and provides a lesson for dealing with our feelings. Christ admitted His feelings and gave His disciples a glimpse of His humanness. *"Then he said to them, 'My soul is very sorrowful, even to death; remain here, and watch with me'"* (Matthew 26:38). Most feelings cannot be ignored; they must be dealt with honestly.

To admit bitterness, depression, or hatred is the first step in learning to deal with how we feel. Christ requested support from His disciples, His friends. He asked for prayer and a watchful response during this dark hour. What a confession of truth He expressed before His followers. Christ understood, in His emotional suffering, that nothing would separate Him from the love of the Father, nor would their relationship be affected by the weight of His anguish. As believers, we need to realize that our acceptance before God is unrelated to our feelings. Trusting in a Sovereign and Holy God is essential in our faith and should not be sustained by the many feelings that dominate our Christian life.

The assurance of joy flows when we fix our eyes on Jesus, " *the founder and perfecter of our faith, who for the joy that was set before him endured the cross, despising the shame, and is seated at the right hand of the throne of God"* (Hebrews 12:2). A new liberty in our Christian life occurs as we realize our faith need not be tied to our feelings. If we live by our experiences only, we may tend to attain our doctrine or spiritual teaching from how we believe. We are assured by His Word that God's presence does not come by feelings, but by faith (Hebrews 13:5b). We don't always have to sense God's companionship to realize the **truth** of His Word.

Lord, thank You for the truth.

(29)

WHAT DOES IT MEAN TO LOVE?

John 14:15 ESV

If you love me, you will keep my commandments.

John, the writer of the Gospel of John, wrote the book with this one thought in mind: *"these are written, that ye might believe that Jesus is the Christ, the Son of God; and that believing ye might have life through his name"* (John 20:31, KJV).

The value or worth we put on someone we love gives us a connection with this person and is the foundation of our relationship. God is our Creator, Redeemer, Provider, and Friend. As a Christian, we have a personal relationship with Him; therefore, we are greatly influenced by His love for us. *"We love him, because he first loved us"* (1 John 4:19, KJV). Jesus is teaching the disciples that no amount of obedience is the true source of love. Genuine love comes from the Father, a gift of love. *"For by grace you have been saved through faith . . . not your own doing; it is the gift of God"* (Ephesians 2:8).

We have believed that our obedience is the proof of our love for Christ and that our obedience will gain us the love of the Father, but obedience does not gain us the love of the Father. His love is a gift given to us when we believe and trust in Him as our Savior. Our obedience flows from this supernatural gift of love that God has given to us.

1 John 2:3-5 says, "*And by this we know that we have come to know him, if we keep his commandments . . . whoever keeps his word, in him truly the **love** of God is perfected.*" Receive Me, follow Me, believe in Me, love one another, trust in Me, and rest in Me are some of His commands. His commands are not burdensome, but trying to keep them perfectly is. Our focus is on our love for Christ as a truly extraordinary gift, because we, as fallen people, cannot obey God perfectly.

Lord, thank You that Your commands are not burdensome.

30

JOY THAT REMAINS

John 16:16-33

In John 16, Jesus is explaining to His disciples that He will be leaving them for a little while, but they will see Him again soon. They are confused by His statement and want to ask Him what He means by it. But, before they can ask, He tells them that they will weep and lament, but the world will rejoice at His leaving. They will have great sorrow, but one day their sorrow will turn to joy––and no one will be able to take their joy from them.

The disciples had faith in Jesus, but despite their faith, they would soon scatter and publicly reject Him in only a few hours. Jesus predicted the disciples' rejection of Him, and God the Father allowed this epic failure in His presence. Now, the disciples' reputation would be known as *the ones who ran away*. The truth is that no one in the history of mankind could ever perfectly love and obey the Lord. The law says, "Do this perfectly and live."

We pursue joy and acceptance in the circumstances of life, but when that doesn't work, we attempt to change ourselves to create joy. Jesus promised to give us something far better: the joy of our hope, eternal life with Him. Jesus said that when He returns He will wipe away every tear, and no one will be able to take our eternal joy from us. We cannot trust in ourselves for joy or put our faith in our self-righteousness, but we can look to Christ and His perfect gift of grace (Ephesians 2:8-9).

Grace looks at our sinful condition and sees that we are not capable of making ourselves acceptable to God. Romans 5:6-10 says that while we were weak, sinful, and ungodly, Christ died for us. God showed His love for us as sinners, and we can rejoice in our Lord Jesus Christ, from whom we have received reconciliation, a joy that remains forever.

Lord, thank You for Your everlasting joy.